CHATTERBOX

CHATTERBOX

A
Conversation
Text
of
Fluency
Activities
for
Intermediate
Students

Peter Voller

Steven Widdows

COLLIER
MACMILLAN

Library of Congress Cataloging-in-Publication Data

Voller, Peter.
    Chatterbox : a conversation text of fluency activities for
intermediate students / Peter Voller, Steven Widdows.
      p.   cm.
    ISBN 0-02-423101-0
    1. English language — Textbooks for foreign speakers. 2. English
language — Conversation and phrase books. I. Widdows, Steven.
II. Title.
PE1128.V66 1989
428.3'4 — dc19   88-23347
                                       CIP

Collier Macmillan Canada, Inc.

Illustrations: Steve Schindler   **Text Design:**   CIRCA 86

Photo Credits: © Minoru Shinkawa (p. 3);   © The Bettmann Archive (pp. 5, 22, 39, 45, 63 — modern art, 65 — The Capitol); © Daniel Simon/Gamma-Liaison (pp. 7, 16);   © Maggie Scarry (p. 9);   © Agatha Lorenzo (pp. 14, 36, 63 — Brooklyn Bridge, 65 — movie theater);   © Eric Liebowitz (pp. 21, 61, 79); © Esther Bubley (p. 43);   © Herbie Yamaguchi and Ryuko Tsushin Co., *London After the Dream* (pp. 50, 51);   © Chris Schwartz (pp. 63 — New York City skyscraper, 65 — token window);   © Frederick Lewis Stock Photos (p. 65);   © Sergio Dorantes/Gamma-Liaison (p. 65 — The Empire State Building);   © Mark Reinstein/Gamma-Liaison (p. 65 — Fisherman's Wharf);   © Gamma-Liaison (p. 65 — cruise ship [French restaurant]).

The Publisher would like to thank the following for their permission to reproduce material that falls within their copyright: Olive Oyl cartoon, © King Features (p. 5); *Time Out* for the personal ads (p. 91); Sandy Smithies and *The Guardian* (27 October, 1987) for the abridged TV guide (p. 97).

Printing: 1 2 3 4 5 6 7   Year: 9 0 1 2 3 4 5

Collier Macmillan
ESL/EFL Department
866 Third Avenue
New York, NY 10022

Printed in the U.S.A.

ISBN 0-02-423101-0

TO THE STUDENT

Have you been studying English for some time, but feel you don't have the chance to use it for expressing your own ideas and feelings? The activities in *Chatterbox* will help you do this. Each unit in *Chatterbox* is about an everyday topic, such as food, fashion, or music, and the activities are designed so you can work together with other students, in pairs, or in groups. Not only will you have the satisfaction of completing a task in English together, but you will also be able to talk a lot about yourself and your ideas, and listen to your friends talking. In short, you will develop your ability to communicate, without needing difficult grammar or a large vocabulary.

Most activities have "useful language" sections, which contain words and phrases that will help you to complete the task. Always read them *before* you start the activity. If you want to use them, you can—they will help you to express your ideas. But *you do not have to use them*, if you don't need them. You may prefer to use other phrases.

Chatterbox is not only about speaking and listening. Some activities contain writing tasks, for instance, making notes that you will use later when speaking to others. There are spaces in the book for writing. Don't write in them until your teacher asks you to. In some group activities, it is better if only one person writes, while the others are thinking up more ideas. For a few of the activities, you will need to tear out the pages in the Appendix at the back of the book. Again, your teacher will tell you when to do this.

Chatterbox will help you communicate more effectively. It will work best if you try to do the following things:

- Take part fully in all the group activities.
- Use only English. If other people in the class speak the same language as you, it may seem strange at first, but you'll soon get used to it, so keep trying.
- Don't worry about making language mistakes: the important thing (as in real life) is to communicate what you want to say.
- If you aren't sure what to do in an activity, *immediately* ask a friend (in English) or ask the teacher.
- Listen to other students and react to what they say.
- Don't hesitate before speaking: your ideas are more important than your grammar.
- Try to give as much explanation and comment as you can.
- Look at the people you're talking to, and don't forget to use gestures.
- Above all, relax and enjoy yourself!

Acknowledgments

We would like to thank our students at Yokohama City University, Tokoha Gakuen University, and Meiji Gakuin University for their help and enthusiasm during the preparation of this book. Also, thanks to Mary Jane Peluso and Lisa Chuck at Macmillan for their work on the manuscript.

P.V.
S.W.

CONTENTS

GETTING TO KNOW YOU

∧Activities in This Unit∧

Circular Introductions

Namecards

Put Up Your Hand If . . .

A Vacation Experience

Find Someone Who . . .

This Is Me!

Getting to Know You

What's My Name?

C·I·R·C·U·L·A·R
INTRODUCTIONS

▶ *In Groups*

Stand up. Form a large circle with seven other students. Follow your teacher's instructions for introducing yourself.

Useful Language

I'm (Peter Smith) from (Los Angeles, California), and this is _____ from
_____. I'm _____ and I (come to school by car), and this is
_____ and (she likes swimming).

NAMECARDS

► *On Your Own*
Write your name on page 141, tear it out, and place it on your desk so that everyone can read it easily.

PUT UP YOUR HAND IF . . .

► *With Your Teacher*
Listen to your teacher's questions, and raise your hand whenever your answer is yes.

A VACATION EXPERIENCE

► *On Your Own*
Think about your last vacation. Can you remember one memorable thing that happened? Write down one short sentence about the event and give it to your teacher. Your teacher will give you another student's sentence.

► *With Your Class*
Walk around and try to find out who wrote the sentence by asking questions.

Useful Language

Did you (eat snails for the first time)?
Tell me about it in more detail.
Why did you . . . ?
What . . . ?
When . . . ?
How . . . ?

FIND SOMEONE WHO . . .

▶ With Your Class

Walk around and ask other students questions using the phrases in the following list. For example, ask "Do you eat yogurt often?" When somebody answers yes, write down his/her name, and ask him/her a bit more about the topic. Remember, you can use a person's name only once, so you will have to talk to at least ten people.

Find someone who . . .

1. *eats yogurt often.*
   (every day? the last time?)

2. *was born in April.*
   (what date? year?)

3. *is wearing contact lenses.*
   (hard or soft? why?)

4. *can play a musical instrument.*
   (what? since when?)

5. *has blood type AB.*
   (blood donor?)

6. *went skiing last winter.*
   (where? good time?)

7. *passed their driving test the first time.*
   (when? easy?)

8. *has bought a record recently.*
   (what?)

9. *had a dream last night.*
   (what about?)

10. *is very ticklish.*
    (where?)

THIS IS ME!

► *In Pairs*

Complete the form on page 143 for your partner by asking him or her questions. Tear out the completed form and give it to your teacher.

GETTING TO KNOW YOU

► *On Your Own*

Listen to your teacher's instructions, and write your answers in the blank spaces in the following diagram.

► *In Groups*

Discuss your answers.

WHAT'S
MY NAME?

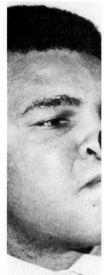

► *On Your Own*

Think of a famous character (living or dead, real or fictional, human or animal) who will be well known to the class. In secret, write down his/her name and some details of his/her life on page 145 of your book. An example follows:

Name:	Ronald Reagan
Age:	Around seventy
Job:	Actor/U.S. President (retired)
Other Info:	Married to Nancy

► *In Groups*

Your teacher will pin a card on the back of one of the students in your group. That student will ask the group questions to find out his/her name.

Useful Language

Who's going first?
Not me! / I'll go first.

Ask questions like the following to find out who you are. Remember, your group members may answer only yes, no, or I don't know.

Am I a man? Am I a woman? Am I an animal?
Am I American? Am I French? Am I Japanese?
Am I dead? Am I alive? Am I a real person?
Am I under fifty? Am I around forty? Am I over twenty-five?
Am I (a sports personality/a movie star/a singer/an actor/a musician)?
Do I write books? Do I sing? Do I act? Do I play sports?
Am I beautiful? Am I intelligent? Am I married?

FASHIONABLE FACES

CLOTHING

► *In Groups*

Write a list of all the different clothes you can think of. Then make lists of patterns, materials, and styles of clothing.

Who's going to write the list?
Not me! / I'll do it!
Give me a word!
How about (socks)?
Good!

NEW CLOTHES, FAVORITE CLOTHES

► *In Pairs*

Ask your partner about any clothes he or she has bought recently, and about his or her favorite clothes. Ask questions beginning with:

what, when, where, how much, and *why*

BACK TO BACK

▶ *On Your Own*

Look carefully at everybody's clothes. Stand up and walk around the classroom. When your teacher tells you to stop, stand back-to-back with the person nearest you.

▶ *In Pairs*

Try to describe your partner's clothes. He/She will ask you questions about details.

Useful Language

You're wearing (a polo shirt).
Yes. / Right.
What color is it?
What's it made of?
Wrong! Try again!
Give me a clue.

S·U·I·T·I·N·G
THE OCCASION

▶ *In Pairs (Men)*

Read these six sets of clothing for men.

A: light gray worsted suit (two piece)/pastel yellow shirt/narrow crimson tie/tan leather shoes

B: mint-green short-sleeved cotton shirt/lemon-yellow cotton pants/sky-blue suspenders

C: cream-colored linen jacket with maroon specks/cotton shirt in small red-and-white check/off-white baggy linen pants

D: black T-shirt with white skull-and-crossbones motif/skintight black leather pants/studded black leather belt/black ankle-length boots

E: gray-green acrylic sweatshirt/faded denim jeans/sneakers

F: Prussian-blue silk shirt/aquamarine tie/dark gray woolen pants/black leather loafers

Below are five different situations. Discuss and mark the suitability of each set of clothing for each occasion. Use the following symbols: 10 = *perfectly suitable*, 5 = *possibly suitable*, 1 = *quite unsuitable*.

OCCASION	SET A	SET B	SET C	SET D	SET E	SET F
Young college teacher giving a class						
Young man at a job interview						
Young man at a disco						
Young man at a baseball game						
Young man going to visit his teacher's home						

▶ *In Groups (Men)*

Compare and discuss your answers.

▶ *In Pairs (Women)*

Read these six sets of clothing for women.

A: emerald-green short-sleeved blouse/white miniskirt/orange socks/white sneakers/straw hat

B: ivory silk blouse/navy-blue collarless jacket/tight knee-length skirt in hound's-tooth check/white panty hose/indigo-blue shoes with medium heels

C: red sweatshirt with geometric pattern/casual white pants/black canvas shoes/lavender cap

D: peaches-and-cream lace cocktail dress/pearl-gray high-heeled shoes/pearl necklace and earrings

E: turquoise pullover/light blue jeans/gray-checked woolen scarf and matching cap

F: loose-fitting beige crepe blouse/pleated olive cotton skirt/brown sandals

Below are five different situations. Discuss and mark the suitability of each set of clothing for each occasion. Use the following symbols: 10 = *perfectly suitable*, 5 = *possibly suitable*, 1 = *quite unsuitable*.

OCCASION	SET A	SET B	SET C	SET D	SET E	SET F
Young college teacher giving a class						
Young woman at a job interview						
Young woman at a disco						
Young woman at a baseball game						
Young woman going to visit her teacher's home						

▶ *In Groups (Women)*

Compare and discuss your answers.

Useful Language

While you are completing the chart:
Which one's best for (a baseball game)?

How about (Set C)?

Is _____ really suitable for (a job interview)?

I guess not. What about _____?

When you are comparing charts:
What did you put for (the disco)?

We thought (Set C) was the best.

So did we.

Hmm, how about (Set D)? Didn't you think it was O.K.?

Well, not really. Would you wear _____ to (a disco)?

FASHIONABLE COLLEGE KIDS

▶ *In Pairs*

Think about the clothes that are fashionable in college this year. Together with your partner, draw a sketch of a fashionable college couple, and label all their clothes.

Useful Language

This year's fashions? Well, I guess _____ are popular.

Hmm, yes. What about _____?

Who's going to do the drawing?

Put a _____ here! Draw a _____ here!

What should we write for this label?

How about _____?

How do you spell that?

FAVORITE COLORS

▶ *On Your Own*

Think of your favorite color. Walk around the class and find other students with the same favorite color.

▶ *In Groups*

Make a list of the things, qualities, images, and feelings you associate with your favorite color beside the Useful Language section below.

> **Useful Language**
>
> Who's going to write down our ideas?
> Not me! / I'll do it!
> What do you associate with the color (purple), (Jim)?
> What about you, (Naomi)?

JENNIFER

▶ *In Pairs*

Look at the song lyrics your teacher has written on the board. Listen to the song, discuss it with your partner, and fill in the missing words. Then draw a picture of Jennifer on the paper provided by the teacher.

▶ *In Groups*

Discuss your pictures.

> **Useful Language**
>
> *In pairs:*
>
> I think this word is _____.
>
> Me too!
>
> Hmm, I'm not so sure. Maybe it's _____.
>
> What do you think Jennifer is?
>
> (It/He/She) might be _____.
>
> *In groups:*
>
> What a good idea!
> Can you explain it a little more?

BEAUTIFUL PEOPLE

▶ *On Your Own*

Choose one of the pictures your teacher will display.

▶ *In Pairs*

Discuss your choice of picture with your partner.

> **Useful Language**
>
> Why did you choose this picture?
>
> Well, I like _____.
>
> What about (her clothes/the colors/his hands)?
>
> Are they important?
>
> Hmm, yes, I think so. They _____.

WHO AM I? (1)

▶ *On Your Own*

Read this useful vocabulary for describing people's faces. The words in each section can fit into the blanks in the key sentences of that section. Here are some examples:

I've got <u>straight</u> hair.

I'm <u>clean-shaven</u>.

I've got a <u>hooked</u> nose.

Hair:

1. *I've got* _____ *hair.*
straight	curly
wavy	shoulder-length
permed	

2. *I've got a* _____.
part (on the left/on the right/in the middle)	
ponytail	crew cut

3. *I'm* _____.
losing my hair (M)	bald (M)

   Hair Color: *I've got jet-black/brownish-black/dark brown/light brown/mousy*/auburn/blond/red/gray hair.*

(M) = Men only
* This word is a bit offensive, so you should be very careful about using it in everyday conversation.

Eyes:

1. I've got _____ eyes.
   - big
   - round
   - sparkling
   - deep-set
   - beady*
   - small
   - narrow
   - sexy
   - bulging*

2. I wear _____.
   - glasses
   - contact lenses

3. My eyes are _____.
   - wide apart
   - close together

4. I've got _____.
   - long/short eyelashes
   - thin/bushy eyebrows

Eye Color: *My eyes are black/dark brown/light brown/hazel/green/blue/gray/bloodshot.**

Face:

1. I've got a _____ face.
   - round
   - long
   - thin
   - pale*
   - rosy
   - triangular
   - square
   - oval
   - tanned/brown
   - coffee-colored/black

2. I'm _____.
   - fair-skinned
   - clean shaven (M)
   - fresh-faced
   - olive-skinned

3. I've got _____.
   - soft features
   - freckles
   - pimples*
   - stubble (M)
   - pointed features
   - dimples
   - wrinkles*
   - high cheekbones

4. I've got a _____.
   - scar*
   - mark
   - beard (M)
   - mole*
   - double chin*
   - moustache (M)

Nose:

I've got a _____ nose.

big*	small
long	flat
squashed*	hooked
straight	cute
bent*	turned-up
Roman	

Mouth and Teeth:

1. I've got a _____.

   small mouth   large mouth

   gold/silver tooth

2. I've got _____.

soft lips	thin lips
red lips	thick lips*
white teeth	yellow teeth*
even teeth	nicotine-stained teeth*
buckteeth*	crooked teeth*

Now make notes about yourself on the form on page 147. Tear it out and give it to your teacher.

FAMILY PORTRAIT

▶ *In Pairs*

Think about a close relative (your father, mother, brother, or sister, for instance), and try to describe him or her to your partner. Here are some questions to help you:

1. *Who are you going to talk about?*
2. *What color's his/her hair? How long is it? What style?*
3. *What about his/her face? nose? mouth? teeth? eyebrows? eyelashes?*

WHO AM I? (2)

► *In Groups*

Try to identify your classmates from the descriptions your teacher gave you.

> **Useful Language**
>
> Who could this be?
> It might be (Mary Jane).
> Yes, I agree.
> But she doesn't have (bushy eyebrows).
> It must be (Doris).
> Yeah, that's right.

DRAW YOUR FACE

► *On Your Own*

Draw your face on the sheet of paper your teacher will give you. *Emphasize your best features!* Give your drawing to your teacher. Then follow your teacher's instructions.

► *In Pairs*

Discuss your partner's reactions to your drawing.

> **Useful Language**
>
> I'm (amazed/delighted/shocked) that you think (I look like a snake)!
>
> Why do you think I look like (a car salesperson)?
>
> Your (first impression/nickname _____) is very (funny/accurate/interesting).

UNIT

3

▲

EAT, DRINK, AND BE MERRY

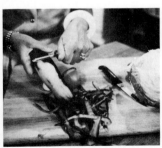

TASTES AND TEXTURES

▶ On Your Own

Next to each quality, write the name of one food that exemplifies that taste or texture.

Bitter	_____	**Sour**	_____
Sweet	_____	**Hot**	_____
Salty	_____	**Sharp**	_____
Bland	_____	**Soft**	_____
Crunchy	_____	**Chewy**	_____
Gooey	_____	**Slimy**	_____

COOKING METHODS

▶ On Your Own

The words in the left-hand column of the following table are all different methods of cooking food. Use your dictionary to check the precise meanings. Then fill in the rest of the table.

	IN OIL OR WATER?	FAST OR SLOW?	WHERE?	EXAMPLE?
FRY				
BOIL				
BAKE				
GRILL				
ROAST				
STEAM				
STEW				

FIND
SOMEONE WHO . . .

▶ *With Your Class*

Walk around and ask your classmates the questions that follow. When someone answers yes, write down his or her name, and ask for more details. Remember, you can use a person's name *only once*.

Find Someone Who . . .

1. *has a food allergy.*

2. *likes hot, spicy food.*

3. *knows what kippers are.*

4. *knows how to make ice cream.*

5. *often eats dinner while watching television.*

6. *knows what food Moslems do not eat.*

7. *had cornflakes this morning.*

8. *drank more than four cups of coffee yesterday.*

9. *loves strong cheese.*

10. *has brought a sandwich for lunch today.*

F·A·M·O·U·S
BRITISH DISHES

► *In Pairs*

Here are four everyday English foods. Try to imagine what they are like, and fill in the table. Do not use a dictionary. This is an exercise in imagination.

DISH	INGREDIENTS	TASTE/ TEXTURE	HOT OR COLD?	COOKING METHOD
Black Pudding				
Shepherd's Pie				
Toad in the Hole				
Bubble and Squeak				

Useful Language

What do you think (black pudding) is?

It might be _____. / I think it's probably _____.

That sounds right! / That sounds horrible!

What about (shepherd's pie)?

TASTING

► *In Groups*

Close your eyes and eat the food sample your classmate will give you. Then write down a couple of words to describe its taste and texture. Compare and discuss your descriptions.

Useful Language

Here you are. Are you ready?
What words did you put for the (first) sample?
I put (sweet, sour, and gooey). What about you?
It wasn't (sour), it was (bitter), I think.

TODAY'S
RECIPE

▶ *In Groups*

Look at the pictures your teacher will give you. They show some parts of how to make a popular American dish. Do not show them to the others in your group. Instead, by describing them to one another, decide how to make the dish. Then display the pictures in the correct order on your desk. Finally, match the instructions your teacher will give you with the pictures.

Useful Language

Who's got the first picture?

I think I might. In my picture _____.

My picture comes before that. My picture shows _____.

What comes next?

Does everyone agree this is the best order?

A LITTLE RESTAURANT

► *In Pairs/In Groups*

Make up a simple menu with your partners. Try to have *original* dishes.

► *In Groups*

Discuss your menus with other groups.

est. 1955

Angelina's

all items available to go

Pasta
Alfredo
Meatball
Sausage
Eggplant
Lasagna
Clams
includes garlic bread $5.00

Pizza
Mushroom, Sausage,
Green Pepper, Salami,
Olive, Pepperoni,
Anchovie, Ham,
Cheese $4.50
Each extra ingredient .50

Sandwiches
"Specialties of the house"
Italian Sausage
Meatball
Eggplant
Salami & Cheese
Ham & Cheese
served with salad $4.50

Salads
Tossed Green Salad $2.00
Chef's Special $4.75
*served with house dressing
and garlic bread*

Soup *of the day* $2.00
includes garlic bread

Desserts
Of the House $1.75
ice cream $1.00
Cappuccino $1.50
Espresso $1.00

Useful Language

When you are looking for a partner:

What kind did you choose?
Shall we work together?

When you are making your menu:

What kind of food/drink should we have?

What about _____?

That's a good idea! Great!

No, that's not original.

When you are looking at other people's menus:

What would you order, if you came to my restaurant?
Well, the (snake sushi) sounds delicious!

A
BALANCED DIET

▶ *On Your Own*

Write down everything you ate yesterday. Give as much detail as possible.

▶ *In Pairs*

Exchange books and discuss your classmate's diet. Evaluate his/her intake of protein, carbo-hydrates, fats, vitamins, and fiber. On the table circle whether his/her intake in each case was too little, too much, or about right.

Protein	too little	about right	too much
Carbohydrates	too little	about right	too much
Fat	too little	about right	too much
Vitamins	too little	about right	too much
Fiber	too little	about right	too much

Useful Language

I think you ate too much (fat) yesterday, because _____.

You didn't eat enough (fiber).

You should try to eat more foods like _____.

And cut down on foods like _____.

Your diet is (not very) well-balanced.

CALORIE
COUNT

► *In Groups*

List the ten foods in order according to how many calories they contain per 100 g. Start with the food that has the most calories.

1. _____	Rice	6. _____	Salmon
2. _____	Pork (lean)	7. _____	Cucumber
3. _____	Beer	8. _____	Oysters
4. _____	Milk	9. _____	Potatoes
5. _____	Butter	10. _____	Potato chips

Useful Language

Which food has the most calories?

I think _____ probably does.

Which has more, (rice or potatoes)?

What about (salmon)?

Let's put salmon (between cucumber and pork), O.K.?

UNIT

4

NINE TO FIVE

△ **Activities in This Unit** △

Job Matching

What's My Line?

What's Their Line?

Good Job, Bad Job

Work Priorities

The Best Job For Me

Man's Work, Woman's Work

Selection Committee

JOB MATCHING

▶ *In Pairs*

Look at the list of professions and definitions. With your partner's help, match each job with its definition. Do not use a dictionary.

Profession

_____ 1. plumber

_____ 2. engineer

_____ 3. social worker

_____ 4. clerk

_____ 5. journalist

_____ 6. sanitation worker

_____ 7. realtor

_____ 8. lab technician

_____ 9. electrician

Definition

a. someone who sets up scientific equipment and helps carry out experiments

b. a person who does paperwork in an office

c. a person who designs bridges, roads, and machinery

d. someone who buys and sells houses and apartments

e. someone who can fix your toilet, sink, and drains

f. a person who collects and reports news

g. someone who takes away your household garbage

h. someone who can rewire your home

i. someone who helps people with family, housing, or other problems

Useful Language

What does a (plumber) do?
What do you call someone who (designs bridges)?
Hmm, I'm not sure. How about this one?
Yes, that must be right.

WHAT'S MY LINE?

▶ *In Groups*

Look at the slip of paper your teacher will give you, but do not show it to the others in your group who will try to guess your occupation. Perform a *short* mime, showing what this person does at work. Answer your friends' questions by saying only yes, no, or I don't know.

WHAT'S THEIR LINE?

▶ *In Pairs*

Your teacher will read three descriptions of what people do at work. Decide what their jobs must be and write down any words that help you decide.

JOB	HELPFUL WORDS
First person	
Second person	
Third person	

GOOD JOB, BAD JOB

► *In Pairs*

Together with your partner, fill in the table below. Choose one job for each of the categories, for instance, a job with a high salary and a job with a low one, a job that's very interesting and a job that's very boring. Remember, you can use a job only once, so you have to think of *fourteen* different jobs!

CRITERIA	HIGH	LOW
Salary		
Interesting work		
Job security		
Status		
Vacation days		
Working with people		
Responsibility		

► *In Groups*

Compare and discuss your answers.

Useful Language

In pairs:

Do you think (a teacher) has a high salary?
Yes, but how about (a doctor)?
Hmm, that's a better idea.

In groups:

What did you put for (high salary)?
Which do you think is the best choice?

WORK
PRIORITIES

▶ *On Your Own*

Look again at the seven criteria for choosing a job (salary, interesting work, and so on).
Complete the following sentences about yourself.

The three most important factors for me would be

1. _____.

2. _____.

3. _____.

The least important factor would be _____.

▶ *In Groups*

Compare and discuss your answers.

> **Useful Language**
>
> Which criteria did you choose?
>
> I chose _____ too!
>
> Why did you choose _____?
>
> Because _____.
>
> What was the least important factor for you?

THE BEST JOB FOR ME

▶ *On Your Own*

Look at the list of jobs. Then, complete the sentences.

• farm worker	• merchant marine	• spy	• copy editor
• kindergarten teacher	• chef	• stripper	• window cleaner
• architect	• zookeeper	• hairdresser	
• police officer	• nightclub singer	• tour guide	

I'd really like to be a(n) _____ *or a(n)* _____, *but I'd never want to be*

a(n) _____.

► *In Pairs*

Now complete these sentences. Don't show your partner—keep your choices *secret!*

My partner would be a great _____, *but would be a terrible* _____.

Compare and explain your choices.

> **Useful Language**
>
> I think you'd be a (wonderful/great/terrible) _____.
>
> Oh, really? Why?
>
> Really! I chose the same.
>
> I'm surprised you chose _____, because _____.

MAN'S WORK, WOMAN'S WORK

► *In Pairs*

Look at the list of jobs.

lifeguard	electrician	doctor	truck driver	judge	gardener
typist	nurse	kindergarten teacher	pilot	office cleaner	sanitation worker

Together with your partner, fill in the table. Which jobs can men do better? Which jobs can women do better? Which jobs can men and women do equally well? Put each job in one column.

MAN'S WORK	WOMAN'S WORK	BOTH

▶ In Groups

Compare and discuss your answers.

> **Useful Language**
>
> Well, (a nurse) is obviously a woman's job.
> I agree. / I don't agree.
> I don't see why a man can't work as a (nurse).
> How can a (man/woman) do such a job?

S·E·L·E·C·T·I·O·N
COMMITTEE

▶ In Groups

Imagine that your school is going to hire a new English-language teacher. Read through the information about the job candidates on pages 36 through 38. Discuss them with your group. Then write down the group's choice, and reasons why the other candidates were unsuitable.

Who's best? What do you think, (Sam)?

I think (Laura)'s best.

Why?

I like (Jeff) most, because _____.

I think (Ted) is unsuitable, because _____.

Yes, but don't you think it's important that _____?

Laura Adams

Nationality: Canadian

Age: 39

Marital status: single

Qualifications: No formal teaching qualifications

Experience and character: Ms. Adams, a successful travel writer, has published *The Philippine Experience* (1984), and *The Best of Bangkok* (1986). She now wants to do similar research in this country. Her teaching style is informal, and she hopes to make some good friends among her students. She has a wide experience of communicating with people from different cultures.

Ted Everidge

Nationality: Australian

Age: 50

Marital status: married (wife is Thai)

Qualifications: B.A. in Education, Melbourne University;

M.A. in Linguistics, London University

Experience and character: Mr. Everidge, a grammarian, has published many articles and books, including: *English Relative Clauses* (1966), *How to Perfect Your Grammar* (1970), *Grammar in the Language Laboratory* (1978), and *An English Grammar for Thai High Schools* (1985). He hopes to find out how grammar is taught in this country. Mr. and Mrs. Everidge have two sons, Nop, age 19, and Do, age 13.

Philip Greg-Smythe

Nationality: British

Age: 23

Marital status: single

Qualifications: B.A., Cambridge University

Experience and character: Mr. Greg-Smythe was educated at one of England's top public schools and studied Icelandic at Cambridge University. He is visiting this country on a government scholarship and will return to England in two years to start a career as a merchant banker. He has no work experience, but he is enthusiastic and wants to observe everyday life in this country.

Faith Miller

Nationality: American

Age: 34

Marital status: married to the Reverend Harold Miller

Qualifications: M.A. in Comparative Religions, Tennessee Baptist College

Experience and character: Mrs. Miller, a Baptist, has lived in Japan and Korea for ten years, helping her husband in his missionary work and teaching English part-time. She believes that one of the main goals of education is the moral guidance of her students. The Reverend and Mrs. Miller have one daughter, Hope, age seven.

Jeff Martínez

Nationality: American

Age: 28

Marital status: single

Qualifications: B.A. in History, San Francisco State University; M.Ed. in
Applied Linguistics, Temple University, Philadelphia (expected
to complete this year)

Experience and character: Mr. Martínez has been teaching at a junior college for the past four years. He got married to one of his students in 1984, but they are now separated. He believes that teaching about the American way of life is an important part of the English teacher's role.

Claudette Nicholson

Nationality: French

Age: 33

Marital status: married

Qualifications: B.A. in English, University of Lyons

Experience and character: Mrs. Nicholson's husband is a New Zealander working for a kiwi-fruit import company. She met him when he was working in France where she was teaching English in a private school. They were married in 1983. She believes that "practice makes perfect" in language teaching. They have no children.

1. *Laura is our choice/unsuitable because* . . . .

2. *Ted is our choice/unsuitable because* . . . .

3. *Philip is our choice/unsuitable because* . . . .

4. *Faith is our choice/unsuitable because* . . . .

5. *Jeff is our choice/unsuitable because* . . . .

6. *Claudette is our choice/unsuitable because* . . . .

THE BEAT GOES ON

∧ **Activities in This Unit** ∧
Musical Variety
Name the Music
Mood Indigo
Sweet Dreams
Writing Lyrics
Musical Instruments
Grammy Awards
Jigsaw Biographies
Local Beat

MUSICAL VARIETY

▶ *In Groups*

Make a list of as many types of music as you can think of on a blank sheet of paper.

Who'll write our list?
I'll do it. Give me a word.
How about (rock 'n' roll)?
Fine. And there's also (opera).

NAME
THE MUSIC

▶ *In Groups*

Listen to the ten excerpts of music. On the table, write in the name of the singer and the title of the song. If you don't know the title, write down any words you hear that *might* be it. Also decide if you like each piece or not, and mark the table accordingly.

	SINGER	TITLE	LIKE OR NOT
1.			
2.			
3.			
4.			
5.			
6.			
7.			
8.			
9.			
10.			

Do you know who the singer is?
Yes, it's (Madonna). / It might be (Boy George).
What's the title?
I think it's (Tarzan Boy). / I heard the words (*she loves you*). Maybe that's the title.

M·O·O·D
INDIGO

▶ *On Your Own*

Close your eyes and listen to the first piece of music. When it has finished, write down the images that the music brings to your mind. There's no need to write sentences; just words and phrases are fine. Then do the same for the second and third pieces.

▶ *In Groups*

Compare and discuss your images.

What are your images for the (first) piece?

I imagined _____.

The music makes me think of _____.

That's a rather (strange/interesting/frightening) image!

Which are the (most common/most striking) images?

SWEET DREAMS

▶ *On Your Own*

Listen to the first part of this pop song. Write down any words or phrases you can remember.

▶ *In Groups*

Compare the words or phrases you wrote down. Then follow your teacher's instructions.

▶ *In Pairs*

Listen to the second part of the song. Every line begins "Some of them want to _____," but what about the endings of these lines? How many different endings are there?

Useful Language

In groups:

I heard (*looking for*). What about you?

Who has the first line?

Maybe I do.

What comes next?

I think _____ comes (before/after) _____.

In pairs:

I heard (four) different endings. What about you?

▶ *On Your Own*
What is this song about? What is the message? Draw your idea on a blank sheet of paper.

▶ *In Groups*
Discuss your drawings.

Useful Language

That's a (striking/wonderful/strange) picture.

What's the connection between your picture and the song?

The song makes me think of _____ because _____.

WRITING LYRICS

▶ *On Your Own*

Choose one of the pictures the teacher shows you, and write a four-line verse about the feelings it gives you.

▶ *In Groups*

Show your picture and read your lyrics. Discuss the lyrics.

Useful Language
Who'll read their lyrics first?
I will.
What do you think?
They're great! / I especially like _____.
I don't quite understand _____.

MUSICAL INSTRUMENTS

▶ *In Groups*

Make a list of as many different musical instruments as you can.

▶ *In Pairs*

In secret, choose the one that best reflects (a) your character and (b) your partner's character, and decide why you think so. Then discuss your choices with your partner.

Useful Language

In groups:

Who'll write the list?

Not me! / I'll do it!

Give me a word!

How about _____?

In pairs:

I think you're (a piccolo).

What! (A piccolo)! Why?

Because _____.

Do you really think I'm _____?

What did you choose for me?

G·R·A·M·M·Y
AWARDS

► *With Your Class*

What are the Grammy Awards? Tell the class some of the categories for which Grammies are awarded.

► *On Your Own*

Who are this year's best singers, musicians, groups, and records? Choose your favorites for each of the categories your teacher has written on the board.

► *In Groups*

Find out the class's opinion by doing a survey. Write down the category your group gives you and their choices. Then get together with the people from other groups who have the same category, and pool your replies.

Group Survey

My category: _____

Our choices:

Intergroup Pool

Winner: _____

Useful Language

For your group survey:

Who is your choice for (best female singer), (Sam)?

(Whitney Houston) because _____.

And you, (Mary)?

When you pool your answers:

Our group had three votes for (Whitney Houston), and two for _____.

So, all together, (Whitney Houston) has fifteen votes, and _____ has seven.

So, (Whitney Houston) is the winner!

JIGSAW
BIOGRAPHIES

▶ *In Pairs*

Here are some facts about three well-known bands. Read the information and identify the bands. Which four facts are about which band? Discuss it with your partner, and write down your answers.

BAND A	BAND B	BAND C
Name:		
Facts:		

1. *Lead singer went solo in 1987.*
2. *Lead singer was born in 1945.*
3. *One band member married a Japanese artist.*
4. *First single was "Love Me Do."*
5. *Vocalist was a transvestite.*
6. *Made "Satisfaction" in 1965.*
7. *Hit the top of the charts with "Do You Really Want to Hurt Me?"*
8. *Manager was Brian Epstein.*
9. *Played in a Liverpool bar called the Cavern Club.*
10. *In the sixties, their image was long-haired, dirty, and immoral.*
11. *Lead singer was arrested on a drug charge in 1986.*
12. *Fan was murdered on stage during an American concert tour.*

Useful Language

I think this is about (the Eurythmics).

No, it isn't. It's about (Queen).

What about fact number eight?

It might be _____. / Couldn't it be _____?

Do you know which band (played at the Cavern Club)?

I have no idea!

LOCAL BEAT

► *On Your Own*

Choose three pieces of recent music that truly represent the best produced in the country/region where you grew up.

► *In Groups*

Form groups with others from the same country/region. Compare and explain your choices.

Select the four that the group thinks most representative, and write them down.

PIECE OF MUSIC	EXPLANATION
1.	
2.	
3.	
4.	

Useful Language

Which three pieces did you choose, (Gary)?

Hmm, I chose _____.

Me too.

Why did you choose _____?

Do you think _____ should be on our list?

How about _____?

That's a good choice!

PEOPLE LIKE US

YOUR BEST QUALITY

▶ *On Your Own*

Check the meanings of the words on page 149. Tear the page out, and then tear it into strips along the dotted lines. Decide which member of your group shows each quality most, and write his or her name on that slip of paper. Use one word for each person in the group, including yourself. Keep your choices *secret*. Then give each person his or her slip of paper.

▶ *In Groups*

Discuss your results.

Which did you get most of?

I got (five *creatives*).

Mine were all mixed.

I feel pretty (surprised/shocked/pleased) that _____.

I didn't know that people see me as (hardworking).

Which did you (expect to get/want to get)?

WHAT'S IN A FACE? (1)

► *In Pairs*
Study this picture.

Now talk about these questions:

1. *What kind of person is she?*
2. *How old is she?*
3. *What's her nationality?*
4. *What does she do?*
5. *How does she feel at the moment?*
6. *Why is she in this place?*
7. *How does this picture make you feel?*
8. *What will happen next?*

▶ *In Groups*
Compare your ideas.

WHAT'S IN A FACE? (2)

▶ *In Pairs*
Study this picture.

Now discuss it with your partner.

▶ *In Groups*
Compare your ideas.

MY CHARACTER, YOUR CHARACTER

▶ *In Pairs*

Read through the following lists of words. Get a friend (or a dictionary!) to help you with the ones you don't know.

Positive Qualities		Neutral Qualities	Negative Qualities
• gentle	• independent	• shy	• gullible
• energetic	• reliable	• persistent	• crabby
• optimistic	• resourceful	• proud	• wishy-washy
• nonjudgmental	• sociable	• strange	• childish
• conscientious	• self-respecting	• sophisticated	• dogmatic
• relaxed	• polite	• careful	• arrogant
• outgoing	• approachable	• ambitious	• jealous
• generous	• patient	• innocent	• haughty
• self-confident	• adaptable	• frank	• stubborn
• hardworking	• has foresight	• impulsive	• greedy
• discreet	• strong-minded	• inquisitive	• selfish
• passionate	• imaginative	• excitable	• sly

Do the following tasks, but keep all your answers *secret*!

Choose five words that describe yourself (include both positive and negative words).

1. _____   4. _____

2. _____   5. _____

3. _____

I wish I were more _____ (one quality only).

Choose five words that describe your partner (some positive, some negative).

1. _____   4. _____

2. _____   5. _____

3. _____

My partner needs to be more _____ (one quality).

Compare and discuss your choices.

Are you ready?

Yes, let's start!

Which words did you choose (for me/for yourself)?

Yes, I agree that (I'm shy/you're impulsive).

But I'm (amazed/shocked/flattered) that you chose _____.

Do you really think I'm (arrogant)?

I certainly do, because _____.

ANGER! SURVEY

▶ On Your Own
What situations make you angry? Can you draw an example on the board?

▶ In Groups
Explain your drawing to the others in your group. Next, read the following questions and share your answers with your group.

Do you get angry . . .

1. *if, in a restaurant, the people at the next table start smoking while you're eating?*

2. *at people who get in your way when you're in a hurry?*

3. *when foreigners say unpleasant things about your country?*

4. *at people who phone you after midnight?*

5. *if shop assistants or waiters ignore you?*

6. *if people stare at you on buses or trains?*

7. *when someone keeps you waiting?*

8. *when you get stuck in a traffic jam?*

9. *when a friend cancels an engagement without giving a good reason?*

Which situations make everyone in your group angry?

▶ *On Your Own*

Choose the *three* situations that make you most angry. Also, try to think of other situations that make you angry. Write them in this box.

1.   3.

2.

Other situations:

▶ *In Groups*

Compare your answers.

Useful Language

When you discuss your drawings:

Which drawing is yours? Can you explain it?

For the first part of the survey:

Why do you get angry if _____?

Why don't you mind if _____?

So, the situations that make all of us angry, are _____.

For the second part of the survey:

Which three make you most angry, (Bert)?

What other situations did you think of, (Spike)?

HOW WOULD YOU REACT?

▶ *In Pairs*

Your teacher will describe three situations to you. After each one, think of and write down as many different reactions as possible for each situation. It does not matter whether your ideas are practical or not; just try to get a lot of possibilities.

1	2	3

▶ In Groups

Discuss your answers. Decide which idea is best for each situation.

Useful Language

When you're thinking up ideas:

I'll write our list! Give me an idea.

You could (sit at home and cry).

Or else you could _____.

Later, when you discuss the ideas:

Which idea is best for situation number one?

I think the best idea is _____ because _____.

I agree. / I don't agree.

I think it'd be better to _____.

AND HOW DO WE FEEL TODAY?

► *On Your Own*

Fill in this chart at the same time every day for a week.

Name: _____   Time of Day:

Day 1 Date: Where are you? What are you doing? Who are you with? How do you feel?	**Day 2** Date: Where are you? What are you doing? Who are you with? How do you feel?
Day 3 Date: Where are you? What are you doing? Who are you with? How do you feel?	**Day 4** Date: Where are you? What are you doing? Who are you with? How do you feel?

Day 5   Date:

Where are you?

What are you doing?

Who are you with?

How do you feel?

Day 6   Date:

Where are you?

What are you doing?

Who are you with?

How do you feel?

Day 7   Date:

Where are you?

What are you doing?

Who are you with?

How do you feel?

► *On Your Own*

After noting your feelings at a set time on seven consecutive days, map out your feelings as in the example of the feeling graph below. Use your own feeling words, arranging them from neutral (on the horizontal line) to positive (upward) and negative (downward).

Name: Peter **Time:** 1:00 P.M.

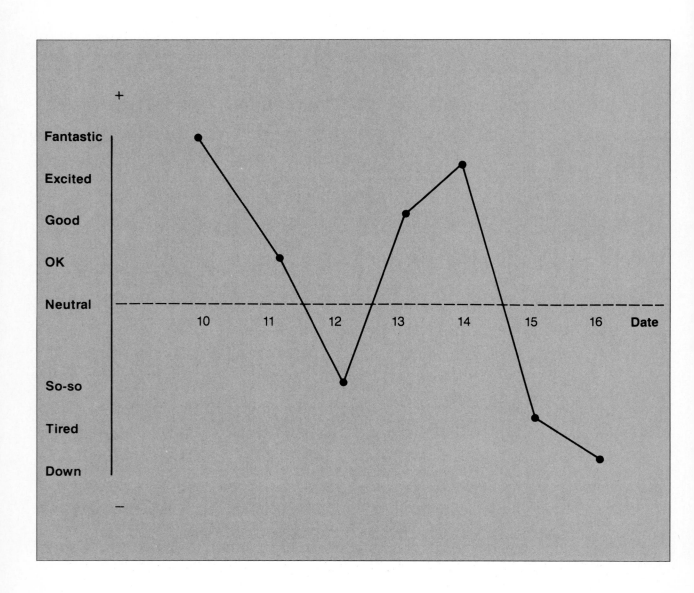

Name: **Time:**

+

Neutral - Date

−

► *In Pairs*

Compare and discuss your **graphs**.

> **Useful Language**
>
> Why did you feel _____ on Monday?
>
> What were you doing? Who were you with?

EMOTIONAL HANDS

► *In Pairs*

Check the meanings of these words, if you're not sure.

friendliness	timidity	dominance	anger
tenderness	passion	playfulness	

Hold both your partner's hands in yours. Close your eyes and follow your teacher's instructions. Discuss your experience.

> **Useful Language**
>
> I thought (anger) was the easiest, because _____.
>
> Me too! / So did I!
>
> I thought (friendliness) was the most difficult, because _____.
>
> I enjoyed doing (timidity) (most of all/least of all).

UNIT 7

GOING PLACES

TRAVEL—
A QUICK SURVEY

► *With Your Class*

1. Ask four friends to name the farthest place they have ever been.

NAME	PLACE

   Who has been the farthest? _____

2. Find someone who has made a trip by plane. _____

   Ask what it felt like the first time he or she flew. _____

   _____

3. Find someone who has made a trip by boat. _____

   Ask how it felt. _____

   _____

4. Ask four friends which of the following they like best:

   a. making trips alone   Name _____ a b c d

   b. with their family   Name _____ a b c d

   c. with one or two good friends   Name _____ a b c d

   d. with a large group   Name _____ a b c d

   Which kind of trip is most popular? _____

NEW YORK IS . . .

▶ *On Your Own*

Write down the images, impressions, and feelings you associate with the places your teacher will name. Here is an example:

New York:
skyscrapers	young	weird people
graffiti	bagels	dancing
subway violence	ethnic mixture	modern art
drugs	never sleeps	Brooklyn Bridge
freedom		

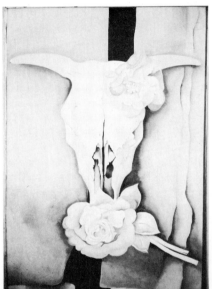

FIRST PLACE	SECOND PLACE	THIRD PLACE

► *In Groups*

Discuss your images and impressions.

Useful Language

What did you write down for (Cairo)?

So did I! / Me too!

Can you explain what you mean by _____?

Why do you think (Paris is snobbish)?

GREAT
<u>DAY OUT</u>

▶ *On Your Own*

Imagine that you are going to _____ for a day out. You will arrive at 10:00 A.M., and you must start back by 9:00 P.M. You can have _____ to spend. How will you spend your day?

▶ *In Groups*

Imagine that you are going to make the trip together. Agree upon a plan.

Useful Language

I'd like to _____.

So would I.

Then why don't we _____?

Well, how about _____?

I'm not very interested in _____.

Will we have time to _____?

DISASTROUS EXPERIENCES

▶ *In Groups*

Look at the four pictures. Your teacher will read how four people describe what happened to them on their vacation. Decide which picture shows which person's experience, writing down any helpful words you hear.

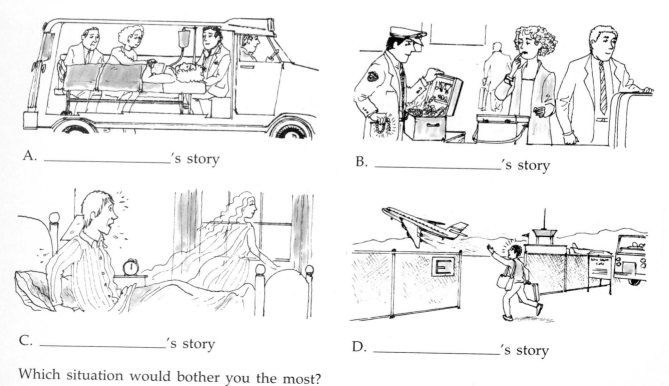

A. _____'s story

B. _____'s story

C. _____'s story

D. _____'s story

Which situation would bother you the most?

Useful Language

Whose story goes with picture A?

Picture B must be _____'s story, because _____.

I heard the words _____ in C's story.

Which situation would bother you most?

I'd hate to _____, because _____.

CAMIGUIN ADVENTURE

► **In Pairs**
Which country is this?

Manila

Camiguin

Map of _____

Your teacher will tell you about a very difficult situation that could happen to a traveler. With your partner, think up as many ideas as you can to deal with it.

► **In Groups**
Compare and explain your choices.

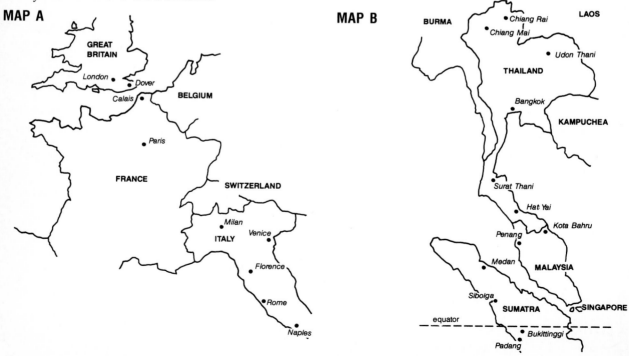

Useful Language

In pairs:

Got any good ideas?

Well, you could _____.

Or how about _____?

In groups:

What would you do, (Sheila)?

But would it really be possible to _____?

That's a good point.

PLANNING A TRIP

► *In Pairs*

Sit back-to-back with your partner. Imagine that you are planning a trip. Look at the maps and choose trip A or trip B. You must choose a different trip from your partner's. Then follow your teacher's instructions.

MAP A

GREAT
BRITAIN

London • ● Dover
Calais ●   **BELGIUM**

● Paris

FRANCE   **SWITZERLAND**

● Milan
Venice
ITALY   ●

● Florence

● Rome

Naples

MAP B

BURMA   ● Chiang Rai   **LAOS**
● Chiang Mai

● Udon Thani

THAILAND

● Bangkok   **KAMPUCHEA**

● Surat Thani

Hat Yai
Kota Bahru
Penang ●

● Medan   **MALAYSIA**

Sibolga
SUMATRA   ●**SINGAPORE**

equator

● Bukittinggi
Padang

Student A's Plan

You work in London, but you have to attend a conference in **Rome** next Monday. All flights are full, so you will have to go by boat and train. You **want to get there** as quickly as possible, so you can do some sight-seeing before the conference **begins**. You can start after your office closes at 5:00 P.M. on Friday. From the office to London's Victoria Station will take at least forty minutes. Plan your trip in four stages as follows:

Stage 1: London to Dover   Stage 3: Calais to Paris
Stage 2: Dover to Calais   Stage 4: Paris to Rome*

*Remember, you must change stations in Paris. This will take forty-five minutes by taxi.

Ask your partner for all the information you need. Plan one stage at a time and complete the following table.

STAGE	TRANSPORTATION	TIME	DAY
1.		dep. London at arr. Dover at	on on
2.		dep. Dover at arr. Calais at	on on
3.		dep. Calais at arr. Paris at	on on
4.		dep. Paris at arr. Rome at	on on

Useful Language

Can you tell me what time the ferries to _____ are?

Do you know { buses / trains / flights

Is there (a ferry) from (Dover to Calais) at around _____ (A.M./P.M.)?

How long does it take?

When will it arrive?

Information for Student A

This is information about *your partner's* trip (Student B). Do not show it to him/her, but use it to answer his/her questions.

Long-distance Buses in Thailand: Going South from Bangkok

Air-conditioned buses leave for the South of Thailand from the Charansanitwong Bus Terminal in Bangkok. Buses leave for all destinations twice a day: 5:30 A.M. and 5:00 P.M.

Approximate travel times to major destinations:
Bangkok–Surat Thani: 12 hours
Bangkok–Hat Yai: 16 hours
Bangkok–Kota Bahru: 18 hours

Transportation Across the Thai-Malay Border

Local buses run from Hat Yai to Kota Bahru (East Coast), but there is no public transportation from Hat Yai to Penang (West Coast).
It is possible to take a taxi in Hat Yai for Penang, and vice versa. The trip takes about four hours by taxi.

Penang–Medan Transportation

Boat service: Suspended until further notice.

Flights: Operated once daily by MAS.
Depart Penang 10:30 A.M. (Malaysian time).
Arrive Medan 9:45 A.M. (Sumatra time).
Flight time is fifteen minutes.

Please note: All flights must be booked in Penang by 6:00 P.M. on the day
before the flight.

Trans-Sumatra Highway Bus

(Medan–Sibolga–Bukittinggi–Padang and vice versa)
Buses leave once a day from Medan to Padang via Sibolga and Bukittinggi.
Departure from Medan is at dawn. Travel times for the three sections:
Medan–Sibolga: 12 hours
Sibolga–Bukittinggi: 12 hours
Bukittinggi–Padang: 4 hours

Student B's Plan

You are a student of anthropology, and you have decided to travel around Southeast Asia during your vacation. After a few weeks in Thailand, you have decided to go south, to Sumatra, because there are many interesting tribes living there. You will travel from Bangkok to Bukittinggi, a small town in West Sumatra. You are ready to set out by Monday afternoon, and want to get to Bukittinggi as quickly as you can. Plan your trip in four stages as follows:

Stage 1: Bangkok to Hat Yai   Stage 3: Penang to Medan
Stage 2: Hat Yai to Penang   Stage 4: Medan to Bukittinggi

Ask your partner for all the information you need. Plan one stage at a time and complete the following table.

STAGE	TRANSPORTATION	TIME	DAY
1.		dep. Bangkok at arr. Hat Yai at	on on
2.		dep. Hat Yai at arr. Penang at	on on
3.		dep. Penang at arr. Medan at	on on
4.		dep. Medan at arr. Bukittinggi at	on on

Useful Language

Can you tell me what time the ferries to _____ are?

Do you know   { buses / trains / flights

Is there (a ferry) from (Penang to Medan) at around _____ (A.M./P.M.)?

How long does it take?

When does it arrive?

Information for Student B

This is information about *your partner's* trip (Student A). Do not show it to him/her, but use it to answer his/her questions.

Train Schedule Between London (Victoria Station) and Dover

Trains leave Victoria Station for Dover at the following times:
5:00 A.M., 5:30, 6:00, 6:30, then every thirty minutes until 9:30 P.M.
The trip between Victoria and Dover takes 1 hour, 10 minutes.

Ferry Service from Dover (England) to Calais (France)

Daily ferry service Dover–Calais.
Ferries leave Dover at:
    6:00 A.M., 8:00, 8:30, 10:30, 12:00 noon, 2:15 P.M., 4:00, 5:00, 7:15, 8:30, 9:30, 10:30, 11:30.
Crossing time is 1 hour, 30 minutes.

Please note: All passengers traveling to France must go through British passport control, therefore passengers should arrive at the ferry terminal in Dover Station *at least thirty minutes before departure time.*

Trains from Calais (Ferry Terminal) to Paris (Nord Station)

Trains leave one hour after every ferry arrives from Dover — e.g., 9:30 A.M., 11:30, etc., until 3:00 A.M.
Travel time to Paris is 3 hours, 45 minutes.
Couchettes are available on all night trains; passengers may occupy couchettes until 7:30 A.M.

Condensed Train Timetable: Paris–Italy

Train Number	0041	0022	0005*	0075	0076	0043	0024
Paris	3:00 A.M.	5:20 A.M.	6:50 A.M.	9:35 A.M.	12:05 P.M.	5:25 P.M.	8:10 P.M.
Milan	12:10 P.M.	1:25 P.M.	10:30 A.M.	4:05 P.M.	9:15 P.M.	2:20 A.M.	4:55 A.M.
Florence	3:55 P.M.	----	2:15 P.M.	6:55 P.M.	1:45 A.M.	6:15 A.M.	----
Rome	7:10 P.M.	----	5:20 P.M.	9:30 P.M.	4:35 A.M.	9:35 A.M.	----
Venice	----	8:35 P.M.	----	----	----	----	11:10 A.M.
Naples	----	----	9:05 P.M.	----	7:55 A.M.	----	----

*Train no. 0005 runs Monday–Friday only.

ANYWHERE
IN THE WORLD

▶ *On Your Own*

Imagine you could visit anyplace in the world. Where would you want to go? Where would you want to avoid?

Five places I really want to go to are

1. _____   4. _____

2. _____   5. _____

3. _____

Three places I'd never want to go to are

1. _____   3. _____

2. _____

► *In Groups*

Compare and discuss your choices.

> **Useful Language**
>
> Which places would you (never) go to?
>
> I'd love to visit _____, because _____.
>
> I'd hate to go to _____, because _____.
>
> But don't you want to see _____?

E · N · G · L · I · S · H
SPEAKING WORLD

► *On Your Own*

Choose any country where English is a native language or is used as a lingua franca. You may not choose the United States or the United Kingdom. Collect lots of interesting information about your country and make a collage, using maps or photos and tables, as well as sentences. Perhaps the questions below will give you some ideas for your poster.

> **My country is _____.**
>
> *What ethnic groups live there?*
>
> *What currency do they have?*
>
> *What is the scenery like? (Any photos?)*
>
> *How much does it cost to get there?*
>
> *Where is the country?*
>
> *What other languages are spoken?*
>
> *What is the climate like?*
>
> *Why is English used there?*
>
> *What kind of food? Any famous people?*
>
> *What kind of government?*

► *In Groups*

Show and discuss your posters.

S·U·R·V·I·V·A·L
ENGLISH

▶ *In Groups*

What are the ten most useful words/phrases for a tourist visiting a foreign country? Discuss, and write your group's ideas here.

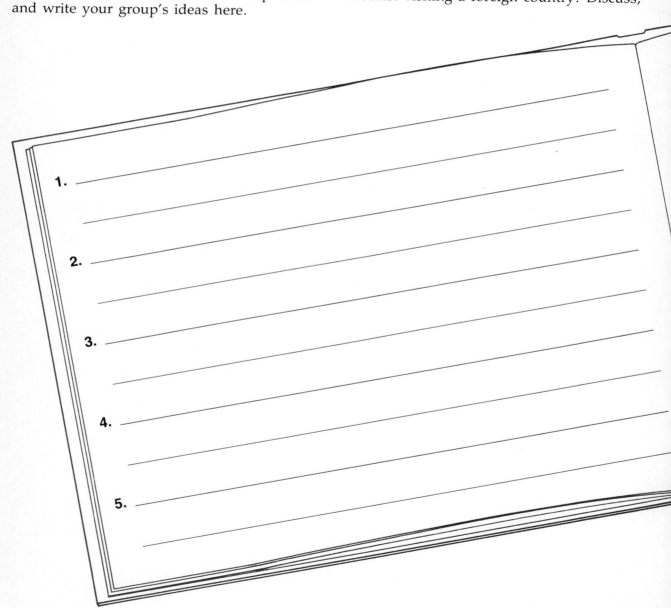

1. _____
2. _____
3. _____
4. _____
5. _____

9. _____

10. _____

HOTEL RECEPTIONIST

▶ In Groups

Imagine you are staying at a hotel in an English-speaking country. You need to say something to the receptionist, but you have temporarily lost your voice (it's only a game!). So you have to communicate your message using mime and gestures. Let the receptionists (your group) guess what you want. You will have to be very active both when you mime, and also when you guess. Your teacher will give you your message; don't show it to anyone.

Useful Language

Just shout out the words and phrases you think the "guest" is trying to communicate. He/She will nod or shake his/her head to tell you if you are guessing correctly or not.

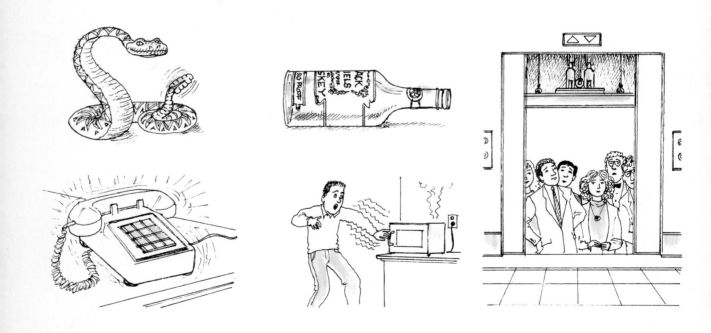

GROWING UP

∧ Activities in This Unit ∧

Golden Days

First Experiences

Cherished Object

What a Whopper!

Teen Problems

Helpline

Cartoon Time

GOLDEN DAYS

▶ *With Your Class*

Walk around the classroom and ask the questions you think are interesting. Ask as many people as possible, and write down any interesting replies.

1. *Can you remember your first day at school? What happened?*
2. *When you were small, did you sometimes fight with your brothers and sisters? What about?*
3. *How much pocket money did you get when you were ten years old? How did you spend it?*
4. *Do you still have any friends left from your elementary school days?*
5. *What did you want to be when you grew up?*
6. *What is the earliest thing you can remember?*
7. *What kind of games did you play as a child?*

Any other questions?

Interesting replies:

FIRST
EXPERIENCES

▶ *On Your Own*

Complete the following questionnaire, writing your age or *never*.

At about what age did you first . . .

1. *go to school (or kindergarten)?*
2. *learn to swim?*
3. *shave (males)?*
4. *put on makeup (females)?*
5. *work for money?*

6. *drink alcohol?*
7. *smoke a cigarette?*
8. *speak to a foreigner?*
9. *fall in love?*
10. *encounter death?*

► *In Groups*

Compare your answers. Work out the group average for each first experience, and say who had each experience the earliest and the latest.

> **Useful Language**
>
> What age did you (first go to school), (Ben)?
> What about you, (Tracy)?
> The average for the (second) question is (twelve) years.
> (Ben) was the latest, and (Tracy) was the earliest.
> Nearly everyone (first drank alcohol) at age (16)!

CHERISHED OBJECT

► *On Your Own*

Bring something to class that has a lot of happy memories for you and that you value highly because of these memories. Be prepared to talk about it, and your memories.

► *In Groups*

Talk about your objects.

> **Useful Language**
>
> This is _____.
>
> I (was given it/bought it) when I was _____.
>
> I used to _____.
>
> It's important to me because _____.

WHAT
A WHOPPER!

▶ *On Your Own*

Think up three stories, *two* of them true incidents from your past, and *one* an imaginary, yet believable, event.

▶ *In Groups*

Listen to each others' stories, and try to guess which ones are untrue.

> **Useful Language**
>
> *When you start telling your stories:*
>
> My (first) story took place in _____ (when? where?).
>
> *When you are judging other people's stories:*
>
> I think the second story is (true/untrue) because _____.
>
> I can't believe that _____.
>
> It sounds unlikely that _____.
>
> It's out of character for you to _____.
>
> *When your friend tells you the answer:*
>
> That's just what I thought!
>
> Really! What a surprise!

T·E·E·N
PROBLEMS

▶ *On Your Own*

Here is a list of problems that sometimes occur between teenagers and their parents. In column A, put a check (√) next to the four problems that you think are the most serious. In column B, put a check (√) next to the four that you think are the most common.

A		B
[ ]	Watching too much television	[ ]
[ ]	How much pocket money they get	[ ]
[ ]	Clothes and hairstyles	[ ]
[ ]	Grades at school	[ ]
[ ]	Keeping their rooms tidy	[ ]
[ ]	Smoking and drinking	[ ]
[ ]	Politeness and manners	[ ]
[ ]	Staying out late	[ ]
[ ]	Making too much noise	[ ]

▶ *In Groups*

Compare and discuss your choices.

Useful Language

Which do you think are the most (serious/common)?

(Smoking and drinking) because _____.

I don't agree. I'd say _____ is more serious because _____.

I don't think (staying out late) is a common problem for boys.

HELPLINE

▶ *In Pairs*

Quickly look through the three letters, and together with your partner, choose the most interesting one. Read it carefully, and then think of as many solutions to the writer's problem as you can. Write down your ideas in the space provided following the letters.

Helpline: The Letters

1. *From Carl, a fifteen-year-old boy:*

I am an easy target for school bullies. I am skinny, wear glasses, and I am no good at ball games. So every week I get beaten up or stolen from. I asked my teacher for help, but he just told me to grin and bear it. Do you have any better suggestions?

2. *From Carmen, an eighteen-year-old girl:*

My parents pressured me into going to college, so I have just started my first year at a junior college in my hometown. I hate it: the lessons are boring, the other girls are nerds, and the teachers are fossils. I want to quit and look for a job, preferably away from home, but when I told my parents, my father shouted until he turned purple and my mother had hysterics. I don't want to break up my family, but I do want to control my own life. Are these two things incompatible?

3. *From Martin, a seventeen-year-old boy:*

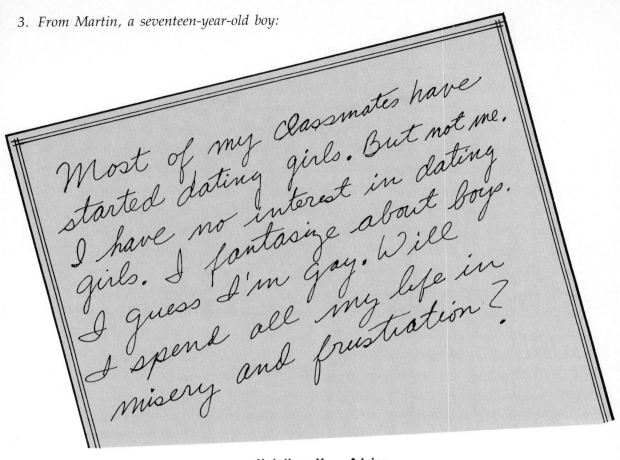

Most of my classmates have started dating girls. But not me. I have no interest in dating girls. I fantasize about boys. I guess I'm gay. Will I spend all my life in misery and frustration?

Helpline: Your Advice

We chose letter ____.

Our suggestions are:

▶ *In Groups*
Discuss your ideas.

When you are thinking up ideas:

I think he/she (should/could try) _____.

Another idea is if he/she _____.

Any other ideas?

Yes, how about if he/she _____.

When you are discussing ideas with another pair:

I think the best thing would be for him/her to _____.

I agree with you. / I don't agree because _____.

Wouldn't it be better for him/her to _____.

Also he/she should _____.

CARTOON TIME

▶ *In Groups*

Your teacher will give you some pictures. Together with the other members of your group, try to arrange all the pictures so that they tell a story. Now write out the story of the cartoon in a simple style that would be interesting to young children.

When you are organizing your pictures:

Which is the first picture?
Perhaps this one.
This picture comes before that.
It shows _____.
What comes next?
Maybe this one.

When you are writing the story:

What should we call (her/her dog/her friend)?
Should we write it using *I* or *she*?
Should we write the story in the past or the present tense?
What word best describes her feelings in this picture?
What's she doing here?

FAMILY AND FRIENDS

M·A·R·R·I·A·G·E
CONSIDERATIONS

▶ *In Pairs*

What factors are important when choosing a marriage partner? Make a list of all the important factors to you.

▶ *On Your Own*

Now look at the list your teacher has put on the board, and choose the four most important factors *for yourself*. Write them in column A.

Now choose the four factors you expect your classmates of *the opposite sex* to choose. Write them in column B.

COLUMN A	COLUMN B

▶ In Groups
Compare and discuss your choices.

▶ With Your Class
Comment on the results.

Useful Language

In groups:

Which factors are most important to you, (Sylvia)?

Which ones do you think the (women/men) will choose?

Probably _____ because _____.

For commenting:

I expected that _____.

I'm surprised that _____.

It's interesting that _____.

WHAT SCHOOLS SHOULD TEACH

▶ On Your Own
Do you think schools should teach about sex? Look at the six topics below, and decide which should be taught in school. Mark the boxes next to each topic like this:

10— It is very necessary to teach this topic.
7— It is probably useful to teach this topic.
4— It is not necessary to teach this topic.
1— Schools should definitely not teach this topic.

[ ] Contraception methods

[ ] Safer sex

[ ] Emotional changes in adolescence

[ ] Responsibilities in a loving relationship

[ ] Homosexuality

▶ In Groups
Compare and explain your evaluations.

Useful Language

How did you mark (contraception), (Calvin)?

With a (1)!

Why?

Well, because _____.

I can't agree. I really think that _____.

Do you really think it's necessary to teach children about _____?

IT'S TABOO IN OUR HOUSE

▶ *In Groups*

Think about the five topics again. Which can you talk about freely with your family and your friends? Which are the most difficult to talk about? Why?

Useful Language

Which topics can you talk about freely with your (parents/friends)?

It's (impossible) to talk about _____ because _____.

At home, we never mention topics like _____.

It's easier to talk to friends about _____ because _____.

I wish I could talk to someone about _____.

TWO
LESS LONELY PEOPLE

▶ *In Groups*

Here are some personal ads from a London magazine called *Time Out*. They were written by people looking for new friends, lovers, husbands, or wives. Quickly look through them and find ones that are interesting.

ROMANTIC MALE, 21, seeks fairy-tale princess for friendship and evenings out. Photo appreciated. Box D350.

ICY bohemian (F) seeks bold genius (M). Box D351.

GEM-QUALITY MALE, 28, handsome, well-cut, scintillating personality, multi-faceted (skiing, karate, equitation, and Francophile), seeks attractive, polished female, 25–35, with the four Cs: character, charm, creativity, and "censuality." Box D352.

GOOD-LOOKING, successful, romantic male, 45, seeks attractive, sensuous, fun-loving female for good times and maybe a whole lot more. Box D353.

TENDER, intelligent woman seeks sensitive man (35–45) to share life. Box D354.

MALE, 28, tall, handsome, humorous, recently uncoupled, solvent, seeks very intelligent, tall, warm, unconventional woman for caring relationship. Photo, please. Box D355.

MID-30s attractive Asian lady (two young children) would like to meet man up to 50. Must be caring and hopefully in a caring profession. Box D357.

LESBIAN, 20, seeks friend any age for happy times. Photo? Box D393.

SINCERE, MODERATELY ATTRACTIVE 5'7" female, 22 years, seeks sincere male. Box D394.

LONELY PUPPY, 20, very attractive, seeks playful kitten. Photo, phone appreciated. Box D395.

GOOD-LOOKING GAY GUY, 30, non-scene, straight-acting, inexperienced, seeks discreet relationship with similar or younger masculine (21 +). Photo appreciated. Box D396.

HANDSOME MIXED-RACE guy, 32, tall, slim, working but poor (no car, etc.), nonsmoker with rock and general arts interests, seeks slim, libidinous (but shy?) lady for genuine relationship. Phone essential. Box D397.

GRADUATE SLEEPING BEAUTY (34) awaits prince, battle-wise, optimistic. All kisses, frogs responded to. Box D359.

BLONDE, suntanned, sophisticated, and forty. Gay guy seeks 24–30-year-old for fun, friendship. Photo, phone helps. Box D440.

DOWN-TO-EARTH COMPANY DIRECTOR, 37, considerate, kind, genuinely sincere, with own house, wishes to meet slim, attractive lady, 28–38, with/without children to share romance and all the nice things in life. Photo, phone no., please. Box D441.

CUDDLY, bearded teddy bear, 26, seeks muscular, straight-looking, handsome soul mate, 21–25, for hugs and friendship. Photo, please. Box D442.

▶ *On Your Own*

Write a similar ad of not more than thirty words in order to find a *new friend*.

Useful Language

What do you think _____ means?

I don't know. Where's your (dictionary/the teacher)?

Which ads do you like best? Why?

This one sounds interesting!

This one's just my type!

A SONG FOR YOU

▶ *In Pairs*

Look at the words in the box below. Make sure you know their meanings; then read them once or twice again.

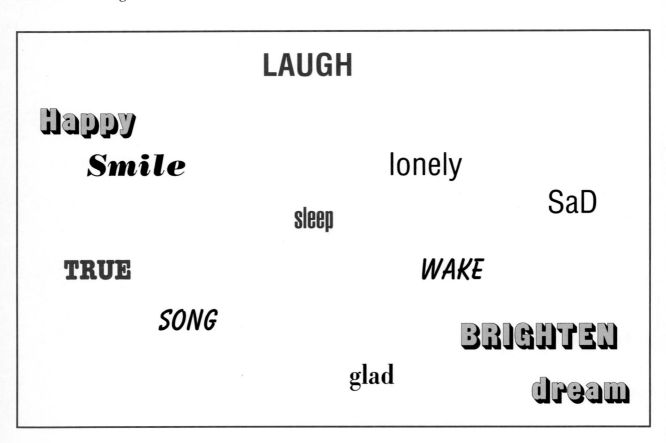

Now close your books and listen to the song.
Look at the words in the box again. How many times does each word occur in the song?

Useful Language

How many times did you hear _____?

Just once. / At least once. / Several times. / Not at all.

I'm not sure. How about you?

▶ *In Groups*

Talk about someone who "brightens your day."

> **Useful Language**
>
> Tell us about somebody who always makes you happy.
>
> (My friend Kay) does because _____.

A DIFFERENCE OF OPINION

▶ *On Your Own*

Read the following opinions, and choose

> the one you agree with most strongly.
>
> the one you disagree with most.

Think carefully about your reasons for agreeing and disagreeing.

1. A girl should be a virgin at marriage.

2. Prostitutes are necessary in today's society.

3. Abortion is murder.

4. It's O.K. to have sex with someone you do not love.

5. Gay people should have legal and social equality.

6. Teenagers should be able to buy contraceptive pills easily.

7. Pornography corrupts people.

▶ *In Groups*

Listen to your classmates' opinions.

> **Useful Language**
>
> I believe that (abortion is murder), because _____.
>
> I don't believe that _____, because _____.
>
> (Sherry) said that she thinks _____.
>
> I'm impressed by her opinion.

A SPECIAL PERSON

► *On Your Own*

Think of someone who has been very important in your life and has influenced you in a positive way. Think about these things:

1. *When did you meet this person?*
2. *Do you still meet this person?*
3. *What did you like about this person?*
4. *How has this person influenced your life?*
5. *Do you have any special memory of this person?*

► *In Groups*

Talk about your special person.

Useful Language

I first met (Gertrude) in _____.

I specially liked him/her because _____.

His/Her biggest influence on me was _____.

I can remember when _____.

∧**Activities in This Unit**∧
Program Types
Screen
Viewing Habits Survey
TV Titles
Soaps
Good, Bad, Interesting

PROGRAM TYPES

▶ *In Groups*

Make a list of as many different types of television programs as you can think of.

Useful Language

Who'll write our list?
I'll do it!
Give me a type of program.
How about (the news)?
Fine. And another.

SCREEN

▶ *In Pairs*

Here is a page of the TV guide from a British newspaper. Read through it quickly, and try to find as many different types of programs as you can. Make a note of your answers next to the TV shows.

Channel 12

6:00 NEWS. Weather.
6:35 REGIONAL NEWS MAGAZINE.
7:00 NO PLACE LIKE HOME. More chaos and crises, with Arthur and Beryl trying to keep the peace between the estranged Raymond and Lorraine.
7:30 EASTENDERS. Yet another episode of daily life in East London.
8:00 LAST OF THE SUMMER WINE: Go with the Flow. Rerun fun with our irrepressible retirees.
8:30 THE LENNY HENRY SHOW. A new sitcom series with Lenny appearing each week as his streetwise, supercool alter ego Delbert, DJ with the kebabhouse pirate radio station.
9:00 NEWS. Weather.
9:30 TRUCKERS: Going Under. Last episode of Jan Needle's road-haulage drama.
10:20 WOMEN OF THE YEAR. Debbie Thrower with highlights of yesterday's Savoy Hotel lunch at which the speakers were Lebanon heroine, Dr. Pauline Cutting, and actress Emma Thompson.
11:00 PURSUIT. Tense thriller with Ben Gazzara as agent trying to outwit the extremist who's threatening a city with deadly nerve gas. 1972 screen version of Michael Crichton's book and his directing debut.
12:10 Weather.

Channel 4

6:00 NO LIMITS: Hardy's Wessex. The rock show goes rural.
7:00 OPEN TO QUESTION. The teenage audience questions the beliefs and practices of white witches Janet and Stewart Farrar.
7:35 ROCKSCHOOL. Another technological teach-in for budding rock musicians.
8:00 FOOD AND DRINK. Chris Kelly opens the new series with top London chef Richard Shepherd, challenged to make Sunday lunch for a group of single-parent families at under $2 a head.

8:30 BRASS TACKS: Bad Habits. John Harrison chairs a discussion between doctors, patients, and drug salesmen.
9:00 THE RONNIE CORBETT SHOW. With Elkie Brooks and Ronnie's sitcom mom Barbara Lott.
9:30 FOOTSTEPS: Pyramids in the Jungle. David Drew mounts an expedition to the jungles of Central America, following in the footsteps of Alfred Maudslay, the Victorian explorer who uncovered the Mayan civilization.
10:20 SING COUNTRY. With Colorado, Mel McDaniel, George Hamiltons IV and V.
10:45 NEWSNIGHT.
11:30 Weatherview.
11:35 ONE IN FOUR. Magazine for the disabled, reporting on one country's attempts to offer integrated living to disabled people.

Channel 5

6:00 LOCAL NEWS.
6:30 THE ROXY. The 21st birthday program with Style Council, Rick Astley, and Black, plus the Bee Gees video.
7:00 EMMERDALE FARM. Yet another episode of daily life down on the farm.
7:30 REPORTING LONDON. With Michael Barrett.
8:00 ALL AT NO. 20: Now We Are Four. Return of the unexceptional sitcom with Maureen Lipman as landlady Sheila, seeking a new tenant.
8:30 BENNY HILL. Highlights of low comedy shows past, with Benny and the gang.
9:00 BOON: Credit Where It's Due. Michael Elphick stars in a new series in this drama as Ken, the two-wheel troubleshooter, his dispatch-rider business going like a bomb, thanks to the two clients at a remote farmhouse.
10:00 NEWS AT TEN. Weather.
10:30 PRAVDA. 40 million readers can't be bad — just good Communists. Documentary painting a unique picture of a paper and a propaganda machine.

11:30 THIS WONDERFUL CROOK. Claude Goretta's comedy thriller, stars Gerard Depardieu as respectable family man with a longing to live dangerously.
1:30 NASHVILLE SWING. With Margo Smith and Jim Owen.
2:30 THREE'S COMPANY: Janet's Promotion. Rerun of same old sitcom.
3:00 MIDNIGHT LACE. Bing's daughter Mary Crosby stars in this 1981 made-for-TV thriller, previously filmed with Doris Day, as heiress terrorized by a mystery phone caller.
5:00 WORLD NEWS.

Channel 7

6:00 BASEBALL: WORLD SERIES. With Martin Tyler.
7:00 CHANNEL 7 NEWS.
8:00 BROOKSIDE. Medical soap.
8:30 4 WHAT IT'S WORTH. Penny Junor introduces another edition of the consumer magazine.
9:00 APARTHEID: 2: A New Order. Second program of the repeated four-part documentary traces the development of, and black response to, South Africa's apartheid policy.
10:00 FOOTBALL. Highlights from an NFL game.
11:15 JUST FOR LAUGHS. A new series of comic turns culled from this year's international festival of comedy in Montreal, with Rowan Atkinson, Wendy Harmer, Roland Magdane, and Mark McCollun.
11:45 REGGIE: It's My Party and I'll Die If I Want to. Richard Mulligan stars in another repeated comedy episode as the eccentric executive, here taking a conservative Japanese contact home to dinner.

(Adapted from an article by Sandy Smithies in *The Guardian*, Tuesday, October 27, 1987).

VIEWING HABITS SURVEY

► *In Groups (Small)*

Your teacher will give you a survey card. Complete it. Then ask every member of your group the questions, and record the replies.

► *In Groups (Large)*

Share your information and complete the report card your teacher will give you.

Useful Language

In your small groups, just ask the questions on your card. In your large groups, start like this:

We surveyed about (commercial breaks), and the replies were as follows:

TV TITLES

► *In Pairs*

Try to match the following four program titles to the program descriptions.

Table A

TITLE	PROGRAM DESCRIPTION
_____ 1. "Dr. Who"	a. Puppet show making fun of famous people
_____ 2. "The Virginian"	b. Documentary about youth unemployment in England in the 1980s
_____ 3. "Spitting Images"	c. Science-fiction fantasy about a man and his time machine
_____ 4. "From the Cradle to the Grave"	d. American cowboy Western

▶ *In Pairs*

Here are two more program titles. Try to guess what they are about.

Table B

TITLE	PROGRAM DESCRIPTION
1. "Watch with Mother"	
2. "The Generation Game"	

▶ *In Pairs*

Finally, here are two more program descriptions. Give them suitable titles.

Table C

TITLE	PROGRAM DESCRIPTION
1.	A documentary about the lives of four young people who were interviewed in 1965, when they were at elementary school; then again in 1975, when they left high school; and a third time in 1985, when they were twenty-eight. It shows how their lives have developed differently.
2.	A program showing this week's most popular pop and rock stars—parts of live shows plus videos.

Useful Language

For tables B and C:
This program could be about _____.

I've got another idea. I think it's about _____.

What title should we give this one?

What about _____?

SOAPS

▶ *In Groups*

Read the list of characters who often appear in soap operas.

Bored housewife	Girl next door	Overworked husband	Boy next door
Perfect mother	School genius	Alcoholic father	Stern schoolteacher
Sweet little old lady	School athlete	Cunning old granddad	Rebel teenager
Local gossip	Motorbike nut	Neighborhood police officer	Amateur musician

▶ *On Your Own*

Assign one character to each member of your group, including yourself. Write down each choice on a separate piece of paper and give the appropriate piece of paper to each group member.

▶ *In Groups*

Discuss the choice of characters.

Useful Language

What did you get?
I got four (alcoholic fathers), so I'll be that.
You be (the local gossip), (Hilda).
I'd prefer to be (the school genius).

▶ *In Groups*

Write the story line for this week's episode of a soap opera. Use all the characters in your group.

This week's episode

What will happen in this week's episode of your soap opera?

Title of episode:	
Location:	Time:
Characters:	
Background:	
What happens in this episode:	

Useful Language

What kind of (drama) should we make?

(When/where) should it take place?

How should it start?

What next?

What if (the old lady and the teacher have an argument)?

Let's say (she pushes him into the pond!).

At the start _____. Then next _____.

Later _____. Finally _____.

GOOD, BAD, INTERESTING

► *In Pairs*

Imagine that, from tomorrow on there will be no more television. What would the consequences be? Think of as many consequences as you can, and write them under the following headings.

Good Effects
Bad Effects
Interesting Effects

Useful Language

Let's see. Under "Good Effects," there's _____.

And also there's _____.

But is that really a good effect?

Let's put it under "Interesting Effects."

A BETTER TOMORROW

PREDICTIONS

► *In Groups*

List as many ways of telling the future as you can.

Useful Language

I'll write our list. Give me an idea!
How about (tarot cards)?
Great! And another!

▶ *On Your Own*

Now categorize these ways of predicting the future under the three headings in the following table.

WORKS	MIGHT WORK	NONSENSE
Total:		

Give yourself *two* points for every method you think works, *one* point for every method you think might work, and *zero* for entries in the nonsense column. Add up your points. The more points you have, the more you believe in predicting the future.

▶ *In Groups*

Compare your results.

Useful Language

Do you believe in (tarot cards)?

I certainly do! / I think (it) might work.

No, I don't! It's nonsense!

Why do you say that?

Because _____.

Who has the (most/least) points?

THE FUTURE . . . IN YOUR HANDS

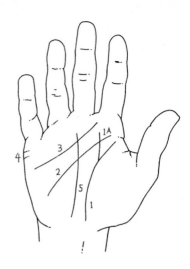

► *In Pairs*

Look at the drawing of a hand, and read the explanation of the "lines." Then read your partner's hand.

Line 1 is your life line: the longer this line is, the longer you will live. Breaks in this line indicate periods of illness.

Line 1A is your ambition line: it indicates when your main goals in life will be achieved. The farther to the right it joins your life line, the sooner your ambitions will come true.

Line 2 is your head line: it indicates how intelligently you will manage your life. A straight line means you will have a "regular" kind of life, but a curved head line means your life will develop in unusual ways.

Line 3 is your heart line: a long, curved line indicates a deep, loving relationship for a long time; a short, straight line means a shallow love life. Any small lines leading off the heart line represent love affairs. If your heart line is very red, then you are a passionate person!

Lines 4 are your marriage lines: the closer they are to the heart line, the earlier you will marry. If you have two or more marriage lines, it may mean you will marry more than once.

Line 5 is your fate line: it is often rather faint, but if you have a clear, strong fate line, it means you will have great success in something.

If your lines aren't very hopeful, don't worry; they may change as you get older!

Useful Language

Example:
You have a very long, curved heart line, so you'll have a deep relationship with someone. But there are also many small lines leading off it, so you'll have many lovers too! You are a very passionate person.

SIGNS OF PROGRESS

▶ *In Pairs*

Put the six events listed into the appropriate column, according to when you think they will happen.

Table A

WITHIN 5 YEARS	WITHIN 20 YEARS	IN MY LIFETIME	AFTER I'M DEAD	NEVER

1. Scientists find a cure for AIDS.
2. Start of World War III.
3. TV phones become commonplace.
4. Cash is completely replaced by credit cards.
5. Doctors find a way to prevent aging.
6. Famine is wiped out forever.

Useful Language

When do you think (famine will be wiped out)?

Oh, probably within twenty years.

What? Impossible! It'll never happen.

Why do you think so?

Because _____.

► *In Pairs*

The four events listed *will* probably happen sometime. Generally, are these good things, or bad things? Mark each number somewhere along the line, to show how desirable you think that event is.

Table B

Good _____ Bad

1. *You can choose the sex of your child.*
2. *New drugs allow people to live to 120.*
3. *Because of new technology, there is no need to work.*
4. *It is possible to travel anywhere in the world easily.*

Now add one other event you would like to see happen in your lifetime.

_____

► *In Groups*

Compare and discuss your answers.

Useful Language

(Joshua), do you think it'll be good or bad (to live to 120)?

Why?

Because _____.

Well I'm not so sure. Have you thought about _____?

I don't agree. I think _____.

SAME PLACE, DIFFERENT TIME

▶ *On Your Own*

Think about the neighborhood around your school: what's it like? Think about the buildings, the vehicles in the streets, the people—their clothes and the things they're doing. Now, close your eyes, and imagine how this area will be in twenty years' time. How will the buildings, vehicles, and people have changed? Write down the changes.

▶ *In Groups*

Talk about the changes you imagine.

Useful Language
What differences did you imagine, (Tony)?
Well, I guess there'll be _____.
And I expect people will be wearing _____.
And maybe everyone will be _____.
Which of our ideas is the most striking?

SAME
PERSON, DIFFERENT TIME

▶ On Your Own

Think about the following questions. Do not write anything.

In five years' time:

1. *Who will be the most important person in your life?*
2. *Where will you be living?*
3. *How much free time will you have in a week?*
4. *What kind of job will you be doing?*
5. *What will be the best thing in your life?*
6. *What will be the worst thing?*

▶ In Groups

Assign one of the six questions to each group member—a different question to each person. Ask your assigned question to everybody in your group, and write down their replies. Compare your answers with other groups.

▶ With Your Class

Report your findings to the class. Think of one more question you would like to ask about people's future lives.

Useful Language

When you compare your answers with people from other groups:

What answers did you get, (Sadie)?

Three people said _____, and two people said _____.

What about your group, (Minnie)?

When you report to the class:

Our group asked ("Where will you be living?"), and the most common replies were _____.

We were (surprised at/expected) this answer because _____.

THE FUTURE . . .
IN YOUR BRAIN

▶ *In Groups*

Many very useful things have been invented in the past twenty years. Can you think of some *new* device that would be very useful? Draw a labeled diagram of your invention on a separate sheet of paper. Show your drawing to other groups. They will try to guess what your invention does.

Useful Language

When you draw your invention:

What about a machine that _____?

Or else a device for (making _____)?

That's a great idea! Let's draw it!

Draw a _____ here! Put a _____ here! No! Like this!

When you look at other groups' drawings:

What a (strange/fantastic/incredible) drawing!

Is it a machine for (making _____)?

No. You're on the wrong track. / Not quite. Try again!

Right!

Let me explain. It works like this: first _____, then _____.

YOUR FORTUNE IN THE STARS

▶ *On Your Own*
Quickly look over the copy of last week's horoscopes that your teacher will give you, and choose the one that seems closest to the way your past week has been.

▶ *In Groups*
Discuss your horoscopes.

Useful Language

Which one did you choose?

What birth sign are you?

Incredible! So am I.

It's completely untrue. Nothing like this happened to me.

It's partly true for me. For example, _____.

▶ *On Your Own*
For next week's lesson: read your horoscope every day, and note whether or not the predictions are accurate.

▶ *In Groups*
Discuss your horoscopes.

Useful Language

Nothing came true for me. What about you?

(A few/Lots of) things came true. For example, (on Monday) _____.

But that happens to everyone.

FORTUNE COOKIES

► *In Groups*

Write your name in the space below, and pass your book to the person sitting on your left. Follow your teacher's instructions.

Name: _____

$$

♡

!!

☆

Discuss your predictions.

Useful Language

I hope my (money) prediction ⎱ comes true.
⎰ doesn't come true. It says _____.

I don't think my (love) prediction is likely, unfortunately!

I'm most surprised at this prediction because _____.

SCHOOL LIFE

∧Activities in This Unit∧

College Facilities

Useful Knowledge

Favorite Hates

Teachers' Styles

Perfect Teacher

Redesigning Your Classroom

College Rules

Teaching One Another

COLLEGE
FACILITIES

▶ *In Groups*

Make a list of all the different facilities in your college or school.

Now make a list of other facilities that you would like the school to provide.

USEFUL KNOWLEDGE

▶ *In Pairs*

Read this list of subjects.

• Computing	• History
• English Grammar	• Fashion and Design
• Classical Literature	• Chemistry
• Current Affairs	• Civics
• Car Maintenance	• Psychology
• Woodwork	• Photography

Decide how useful it is, *in everyday life*, to know about each subject. Then, write down each subject under one of the headings in the table.

VERY USEFUL	SLIGHTLY USEFUL	USELESS
Total: _____ years	_____ years	_____ years

Useful Language

Which column did you put (photography) in?

"Very Useful." What about you?

Why do you think it's so useful?

Well, because _____.

▶ *In Pairs*

Now, in the previous table, write down next to each subject how many years you studied it in high school. If you didn't study a subject, put 0. Add up the figures in each column, and write the totals at the bottom of the table. Finally, think of two other subjects that you think would be useful, but which you didn't study at school.

1. _____   2. _____

▶ *In Groups*

Compare and discuss your findings.

Useful Language

What's your total number of years for (useless)?
(25!) What do you think this proves?
Overall, how useful were our high school years?
What other useful subjects did you write down, (Brian)?

FAVORITE HATES

▶ *With Your Class*

Think about the subjects you studied at school. Which was your favorite? Why? Walk around and ask other students.

Now, do the same, asking which did you hate most?

▶ *In Groups*

Discuss the reasons for your choices.

Useful Language

Which subject did you (like/hate) most in high school?

Oh, me too!

Hmm, mine was _____.

Why did you (like/hate) (English)?

Because _____.

In my case because _____.

TEACHERS' STYLES

▶ *On Your Own*

Choose one teacher and observe his/her behavior during one lesson. Make a note of the following points:

Type of class (e.g., lecture/seminar): _____

Number of students: _____

1. Where does the teacher stand (or sit) during the lesson?

2. How much does he/she move around the classroom? Where to?

3. How much eye contact does he/she make with students?

4. If the teacher speaks to a student, how does he/she address the student? (By name/ By pointing/Some other way?)

5. How much dialogue is there between teacher and student? (A lot/A little/None?)

► *In Groups*

Compare and discuss your answers to the questionnaire.

> **Useful Language**
>
> What type of lesson did you observe?
>
> Where did the teacher stand?
>
> What did you like (most/least) in (his/her) lesson?
>
> Do you think it's important to (make eye contact)?
>
> Yes, because _____.
>
> Not really, because _____.
>
> I (don't) like it when the teacher points, because _____.

P·E·R·F·E·C·T
TEACHER

► *On Your Own*

What is a good college teacher like? Put the following qualities in order, from 1 (the least essential) to 9 (the most essential).

[   ] Maintains strong discipline and control.

[   ] Knows his/her subject thoroughly, and keeps up to date.

[   ] Really likes his/her students and socializes with them outside the class.

[   ] Tries to give his/her students moral guidance.

[   ] Tries to make the lessons interesting and fun.

[   ] Shares his/her own ideals and experiences with the students.

[   ] Treats all students fairly and does not have favorites.

[   ] Makes the students work hard in and out of class.

[   ] Encourages the students to think for themselves, and to study on their own.

Now add one more quality that you think is important in a college teacher.

▶ *In Groups*

Compare your rankings. Produce a group ranking by totaling each student's ranking for each quality.

Useful Language

What did you put (first/next/last)?

Why did you put (*maintains strong discipline*) (so high/so low)?

I see your point, but I think _____.

Where did you rank (*knows his/her subject thoroughly*), (Peter)?

So, our group ranking looks like this. First _____, second _____.

What other quality did you think of, (Janice)?

REDESIGNING YOUR CLASSROOM

▶ *In Pairs*

How could you improve your classroom? Look at the diagram that your teacher will give you. With your partner, try to write as many alternative ideas for each feature of the class-room as you can. Be imaginative! Add any new features that you would like the room to have.

▶ *In Groups*

Share your ideas with another pair, and then, in fours, draw a labeled diagram of your rede-signed classroom.

Useful Language

What could we have instead of (desks in rows)?

How about (chairs in a semicircle)?

Or what about _____?

Let's add a _____ here!

Let's have (a pink wool carpet) instead of (a concrete floor).

Fine! What else?

COLLEGE
RULES

▶ *In Pairs*

Think about the rules at your college or school, and choose two that are necessary, and two that are unnecessary.

▶ *In Groups*

Discuss your choices. Decide on three useful and three useless rules.

▶ *In Pairs*

Choose one of the useless rules. Discuss how to change it.

Useful Language

In pairs:

Let's see, what rules do we have?

There's (no smoking in the classroom) and also _____.

Do you think that rule is necessary?

Yes, I do, because _____.

Not really. I don't see why _____.

In groups:

Which (un)necessary rules did you choose?

Which are the most (un)necessary, do you think?

In pairs:

Which rule would you most like to change?

How could we change it?

TEACHING ONE ANOTHER

▶ *On Your Own*

Think of a simple thing that you can do, which you could teach somebody in a few minutes. Prepare a five-minute presentation of this skill for the *next class time*.

▶ *In Groups*

Take turns teaching one another your skill.

Useful Language

Who'll go first?

Not me! / O.K., I will!

I'm going to (show/teach) you how to _____.

First _____, then _____, now try to _____.

Do it like this.

Good.   O.K.   You've got it.

BEAUTIFUL BODIES

STAND UP! SIT DOWN!

► *With Your Class*

Stand up, form a big circle with your classmates, and follow your teacher's instructions.

PARTS OF THE BODY

► *In Pairs*

Look at the two pictures below, and label the various parts of the body as indicated, using the following words.

ankle   arm   toes   thigh   wrist   stomach   calf   waist

shoulder   knee   groin   neck   elbow   chest   hip

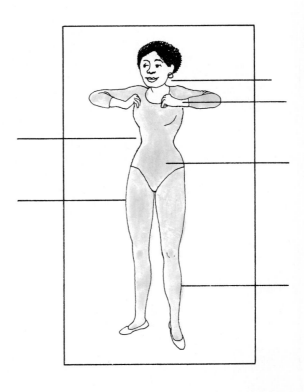

THE
TALLEST, LONGEST, BIGGEST

▶ *In Groups*

Choose a question from the list your teacher will write on the board. Then ask every member of the class your group's question. Write down their replies on the chart on page 128.

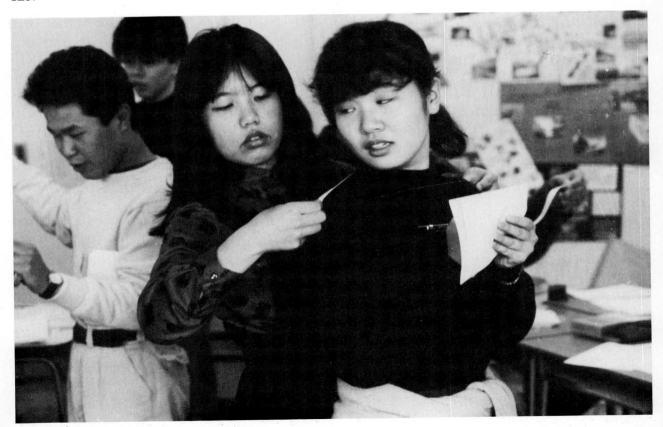

My question is _____

Students' Names   **Replies**

(Men)

Student's Names   **Replies**

(Women)

Compare your information. Work out average measurements, one for the women, one for the men. Find out the biggest and smallest measurements.

(Troy), you ask the following students (Jan, Mike, _____).
Can you tell me (what size shoes you wear)?
May I measure you?

When comparing your answers:

What are your answers, (Troy)?
So, the averages are (155 pounds) for the guys, and (118 pounds) for the women.
So, (Joe — size 12, and Julie — size 8) have the (biggest feet)!

WHO AM I?

▶ *On Your Own*

Read through the following words that describe people's bodies, and then make notes about yourself on the form on page 151. The words in each section can fit together as in these examples:

> *I have thin arms.*
> *I have thick, hairy thighs.*
> *I have round shoulders.*

I have a	large hairy compact flabby		slim smooth powerful muscular		body
I have a(n)	**Men** broad narrow beefy puny hairy	chest	**Women** large small average-sized		bust
I have		broad narrow round bony			shoulders

I have a	flat muscular flabby bulging huge	stomach
I have a	slim narrow bulging	waist
I have a	large well-rounded flat sexy	behind
I have	short long thin thick muscular sinewy fat hairy	legs arms calves thighs
I have	knobby	knees elbows
I have	big small delicate tough	hands feet

Some of the words in this chart may be considered offensive, so you should be very careful about using them in everyday conversation.

Your teacher will collect your description form.

► *In Groups*

Try to identify the descriptions you have.

Who could this be?
It might be (Jay).
Yes, perhaps. But he doesn't have a (beefy chest)!
So then, it might be (Gordon).
Yes, I agree. He certainly has (muscular thighs) too!

YOU MUST BE . . .

▶ *On Your Own*

Check through the vocabulary for bodies again.

▶ *In Pairs*

Then stand up and follow your teacher's instructions.

Example:

You have short . . . muscular . . . quite hairy arms . . . broad shoulders . . . a flat
stomach . . . and . . . big hands. You must be (Mickey)!

LIFETIME
FITNESS

▶ *In Pairs*

A man in his twenties can expect to live to age seventy-four. A woman in her twenties can
expect to live to age seventy-seven. However, many factors affect these averages. Ask your
partner the following questions. When he/she answers yes, give him/her the points indicated
next to that question. At the end, add up the total number of points, and add (or subtract!)
it from the average, to find out how long he/she will live!

	YES	PARTNER'S SCORE
Have any of your grandparents lived to 80 or more?	+1	
Has anyone in your family died of a heart attack, a stroke, or cancer?	−3	
Do you smoke . . . more than 40 cigarettes a day? 20 to 40 cigarettes a day? less than 20 cigarettes a day? not at all?	−12 −7 −3 0	
Do you hug someone nearly every day?	+2	
Do you often sleep more than 10 hours a night?	−2	
Do you often sleep less than 5 hours a night?	−2	
Do you drink more than 5 cups of tea or coffee a day?	−1	
Do you eat fresh fruit or vegetables every day?	+4	
Do you eat candy, cake, or chocolate . . . every day? sometimes?	−2 −1	
Do you live alone?	−4	
Do you exercise . . . at least three times a week? once or twice a week?	+4 +2	
Do you go away on vacation twice or more every year?	+2	
Do you drink more than two bottles of beer, or two whiskies, a day?	−6	
Do you study and/or work more than 10 hours a day?	−3	
	Total	_____

My partner can expect to live to the age of _____.

DON'T
TOUCH ME THERE!

▶ *On Your Own*

There are unwritten rules about where we may, and may not, touch other people. Look at the diagrams below, and shade them as follows:

You *never* touch people here.

You *sometimes* touch people here.

You *quite often* touch people here.

You *often* touch people here.

Mother	Father	Female Friend	Male Friend

▶ *In Groups*

Compare and discuss your diagrams.

Useful Language

How did you shade the (female friend, Freddie)?

I shaded the hair and face (*sometimes*), the shoulders (*often*), _____.

Mine's different. I shaded _____.

I think it's alright/common/unusual to touch (your father's legs).

Are there any differences between the men's and the women's answers?

Who touches people most/least?

BODY LANGUAGE

▶ *In Pairs*

People's facial expressions and body postures can tell us a lot about what they are thinking. Look at the six pictures, and try to match each of the following six thoughts to the most appropriate picture.

1. *I'm telling a lie.*
2. *I need time to consider your idea.*
3. *I want to be completely honest with you.*
4. *I think I'm smarter than you.*
5. *I'm nervous but trying to hide it.*
6. *I think you're too boring and unimportant to bother with.*

A
B
C
D
E
F

▶ *In Groups*

Compare your answers.

Useful Language

In pairs:

What about (A)? What do you think he's thinking?

Which one do you think is (telling a lie)?

I think it's (B) because _____.

But look at his (hands/posture/_____).

In groups:

What did you put for (A)?

Yes, we chose the same.

Hmm, we don't agree. We think _____ because _____.

KEEPING FIT

▶ *In Groups*

Look at the six drawings, and match them with the following six labels.

- push-up
- back stretch
- groin stretch
- ankle stretch
- bent-knee sit-up
- calf and thigh stretch

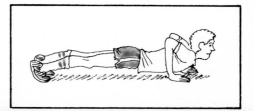

Useful Language

I think this is the (*calf and thigh stretch*). Do you agree?
Hmm, yes. / Hmm, no. Surely that's the (*back stretch*)!
But that exercise doesn't (stretch your back)!

► *In Groups*

Now choose five of the movements in the table, and mime them for your group. When your friends do their mimes, guess which movements they are miming, and check them on the list.

MOVEMENTS	NAME	NAME	NAME	NAME
Stretch your arms				
Kneel down				
Twist your hips				
Swing your arms				
Bend forward				
Bend backward				
Lift a leg				
Turn your head				
Bend your knees				
Lie on your back				
Lie on your stomach				
Stand on tiptoe				
Bring your legs together				
Stand with your feet apart				
Touch your toes				

MOVEMENTS	NAME	NAME	NAME	NAME
Raise an arm				
Flex your upper arms				
Shake your hands				
Expand your chest				
Sway from side to side				

Check your answers with one another.

Useful Language

What did I do?
First, you (twisted your hips), right?
Right! Then, what next?
Next, you (bent forward).
No, sorry. Try again.

APPENDIX

Unit 1: Namecards

* * * * * Fold here * * * * *

Write your name clearly inside the box. Use colors if you can.

* * * * * Fold here * * * * *

Unit 1: **THIS IS ME!**

Last Name _____

First Name _____

Birthday _____

Age _____

Address _____

_____

_____

_____

Phone No. _____

Hobbies and Interests:

Affix photo

Unit 1: What's My Name?

Name:

Age:

Job:

Other Info:

Unit 2: Who Am I?

Hair (color/length/style):

Eyes (color/shape/eyelashes/eyebrows):

Face (shape/complexion/other features):

Nose (shape/size):

Mouth and Teeth (size/shape/color):

Unit 6: **Your Best Quality**

sophisticated
gentle
energetic
sensitive
generous
hardworking
brave
sexy
cheerful
creative

Unit 13: Who Am I?

Body (body/chest/shoulders):

Body (stomach/waist/behind):

Legs (thighs/calves/knees/feet):

Arms (arms/elbows/hands):